football

ian howe

A CONNECTIONS • AXIS EDITION

A Connections • Axis Edition

This edition first published in Great Britain by
Connections Book Publishing Limited
St Chad's House
148 King's Cross Road
London WC1X 9DH
and Axis Publishing Limited
8c Accommodation Road
London NW11 8ED
www.axispublishing.co.uk

Conceived and created by
Axis Publishing Limited

Creative Director: Siân Keogh
Managing Editor: Brian Burns
Project Designer: Anna Knight
Project Editor: Madeleine Jennings
Production Manager: Sue Bayliss
Photographer: Mike Good

Note
The opinions and advice expressed in this book
are intended as a guide only. The publisher and
author accept no responsibility for any injury
or loss sustained as a result of using this book.

British Library Cataloguing-in-Publication data
available on request.

ISBN 1–85906–098–6

9 8 7 6 5 4 3 2 1

Separation by
United Graphics Pte Limited
Printed and bound by
Star Standard (Pte) Limited

a *flowmotion* title**

football

contents

introduction

FOOTBALL is one of the most popular team games in the world. The spread of both the men's and women's game has been helped hugely by the amount of media coverage given to the sport, with professional games from all over the world transmitted to all households with a television.

Every skill seen on our televisions started somewhere; a training ground, playground, local park or even a clumsy first attempt in the backyard. People play sports for a variety of reasons, ranging from fun, competition, a way of keeping fit, or purely as a social activity where they can meet new friends. All sports provide enjoyment, fitness and the learning of new skills, which, in most cases, are different from the skills used in everyday life.

Whatever the individual reason for taking up football, there is always room for improvement. Professional and amateur players are constantly striving to enhance their abilities on the field, and this requires a well-balanced training programme. For years, ordinary coaching manuals using ordinary photographs failed to show the key point of every movement. By studying the sequence of photographs in this book and copying the body shapes and foot movements, you can easily enhance your skills and develop new ones.

WARMING UP Always warm up before a training session to get the blood pumping around you body and to help prevent injuries. Try lifting one leg at a time and lightly touching the top of a stationary ball with the soles of your boots (left) or keeping on your toes while passing the ball between your feet (far left).

what is a skill?

By definition, a football skill is a series of interlinked moves that requires special ability or expertise. It also requires special training. There is a beginning, middle and end to each skill, and these can be practised individually, then put together and practised in their entirety.

Learning skills should be fun, so do not work on one exercise for more than 15 minutes at a time. Always move onto a new activity before you tire of the old one. An entire skills training session should not exceed 1 hour for players under 10 years of age.

This book concentrates on the following basic skills:

1. CONTROLLING
2. PASSING
3. DRIBBLING
4. TURNING
5. SHOOTING
6. HEADING
7. GOALKEEPING

As the game becomes more competitive, technical, and physical, all players – regardless of their position on the pitch – require a broader range of skills. Defenders need to learn how to receive the ball at any height or angle, bring it under control and progress play, just as strikers need to learn defensive moves. So, aim to make learning new skills an enjoyable part of training sessions.

putting skills into practice

Once you have become familiar and competent with each of the different football skills, you need to learn when to use them. Do not use a complicated skill when there is a simpler alternative.

Before you even come into contact with the ball, you need to ask yourself questions: Am I in danger of losing the ball? Do I need to use a defensive skill? Are there team mates nearby? Can I pass the ball? Is the path clear to run with the ball? Can I aim for the goal? Deciding what skill to use when is what makes a good player.

practice makes perfect

With quality practice sessions you should see improvements in your skills within a six-month period. Monitor your skills and fitness level on a simple chart (see opposite). For instance, if you are practising turns, time yourself for one minute over five metres to see how many you can make. Record the result and check in a week's time over the   same distance for the same amount of time. If you do just one more, you know you are improving.

START OFF SLOW Always start each section of a training skill at a walking pace. Pay specific attention to your body shape and the part of the foot (contact surface) you need to use to play the ball. As you become more confident and comfortable with the moves, you can pick up the pace.

KEEPING RECORDS

SKILL	THE CHALLENGE	DURATION	DATE / SCORE	DATE / SCORE	DATE / SCORE	DATE / SCORE
turns	turn between two cones 5m apart	1 minute	1/1/02 10	8/1/02 11	15/1/02 12	22/1/02 11
passing	working with a friend passing through cones 10m apart	1 minute	1/1/02 20	8/1/02 22		
heading						
shooting						
dribbling						

If you are not improving at a particular skill, don't worry. Just go back over it section by section, trying to identify the parts of the skill that you need to improve on, and work on those again. Remember always to set yourself achievable targets – it goes hand in hand with skills improvements.

play safe

Over-training is just as bad as not training enough. Many young football players suffer burnout by playing in too many games, accompanied by excessive training over a short period. You should always rest between games and training sessions to achieve your maximum level of performance.

Other things to bear in mind include wearing the appropriate protective clothing (see page 8–9). You should not practise if conditions are wet, or if you are unwell, tired or injured. Always wait until you have fully recovered, otherwise you may cause a long-term repetitive injury.

ball trajectories

Experiment with the ball and you will find that you can create different movements by striking the ball at different angles with different parts of the foot. For example, striking the right side of the ball with the inside of your right foot will bend the ball left. Striking the left side of the ball with the outside of your right foot will bend the ball right. And striking the ball underneath will send it spiralling up.

equipment

footwear

Wearing the appropriate boots or training shoes is very important when practising football skills. Different surfaces and weather conditions require different kinds of footwear. Choosing the right one will help you maximise your skills on the pitch and avoid any injuries.

Choose footwear for comfort and safety, not for colour or any other style aspect. Make sure you wear the correct size – ill-fitting ones can cause long-term injuries.

PLAYING ON CONCRETE Wear trainers that have a flat surface and good tread. If it has been raining, the surface may be slippery so always check before you start to train or play a game. Do not attempt to train if puddles are still visible on concrete surfaces.

PLAYING ON SOFT GROUND Wear football boots with changeable studs. Keep an eye out for uneven wear of studs and immediately replace any that become sharp on an edge. A new blade system of boots can also be worn on soft ground. Always keep boots clean in between matches because untidiness can reflect on your performance.

A basic pair of trainers with flat surfaces and good tread should be worn on concrete and indoor surfaces.

Astro turf boots are good to wear when playing on hard ground.

PLAYING ON GRASS In the summer when playing grounds become hard, wear sturdy trainers, astro turf boots, or short multi-stud system boots.

the ball
Always make sure that the ball you choose is not too big or heavy for the players. Below is a recommended guideline.

UNDER 9 YEARS OF AGE	**SIZE 3**
9 TO 14 YEARS OF AGE	**SIZE 4**
OVER 14 YEARS OF AGE	**SIZE 5**

shin pads
These should be worn during all games and practices whenever there is contact between two players. It is illegal to play in matches without shin pads and players will be sent off for failure to do so. Some pads slip down behind the sock, but others with ankle protectors need to be put on before socks. Choose your pads wisely for comfort and maximum protection.

markers
You can buy simple markers from sports retailers but any suitable object can be used to set up working grids for training.

Never use sharp or fragile objects as markers for obvious safety reasons.

goalkeeper's outfit
In addition to shin pads, goalkeepers also have the option of wearing shirts and shorts with built-in padding. This helps to soften the impact when diving towards a ball.

Goalkeeping gloves come in many different varieties and vary hugely in price. Choose a pair that fit well and tighten around the wrist as this prevents them from falling off. They should have good grip on the palms where they come into contact with the ball. Some gloves now have reinforced fingers for added protection, but these are much more expensive than normal ones.

Shin pads are an essential part of your football kit.

stretching

Always warm up your muscles with 10 minutes of stretching before a training session. Equally important is a cooling down stretch session once you have finished. Stretching has the following benefits. It:

- Prepares the body for activity, signalling to your brain that your muscles are about to be used.
- Reduces muscle tension by making the body more relaxed

- Improves co-ordination and increases range of motion.
- Prevents muscle strains (a strong pre-stretched muscle resists stress better than a strong, unstretched muscle) and repetitive injuries.
- Helps to create body awareness.
- Promotes circulation.

Twisting from side to side with your feet planted to the ground will stretch your hips and lower back.

Bending forwards with your weight on your front leg will stretch your calf muscles.

Leaning forwards to touch your toes will stretch your hamstring muscles.

Practise with a partner by standing back to back and passing the ball. This will stretch your hips.

go with the flow

Flowmotion is a revolutionary photographic coaching system. In a series of detailed photographs, it shows every movement and body shape used in basic football skills and not just the selected highlights. This enables the reader to teach themselves with far more accuracy, without the presence of a coach. Just by following the step-by-step Flowmotion pages, you can improve and learn new skills in your own time. The captions along the bottom of the images provide additional information to help you perform the skills confidently. Below this, another layer of information includes basic instructions and symbols indicating when to move forward. On pages 49, 80, 81, 84 and 85, the blue marker represents the player's opponent.

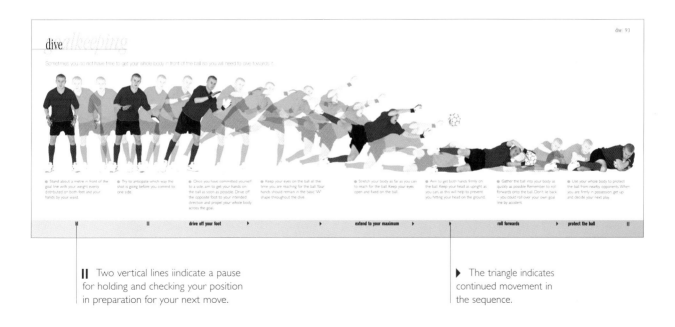

dive *goalkeeping*

dive | 93

Sometimes you do not have time to get your whole body in front of the ball so you will need to dive towards it.

● Stand about a metre in front of the goal line with your weight evenly distributed on both feet and your hands by your waist.

● Try to anticipate which way the shot is going before you commit to one side.

● Once you have committed yourself to a side, aim to get your hands on the ball as soon as possible. Drive off the opposite foot to your intended direction and propel your whole body across the goal.

● Keep your eyes on the ball all the time you are reaching for the ball. Your hands should remain in the basic 'W' shape throughout the dive.

● Stretch your body as far as you can to reach for the ball. Keep your eyes open and fixed on the ball.

● Aim to get both hands firmly on the ball. Keep your head as upright as you can, as this will help to prevent you hitting your head on the ground.

● Gather the ball into your body as quickly as possible. Remember to roll forwards onto the ball. Don't lie back – you could roll over your own goal line by accident.

● Use your whole body to protect the ball from nearby opponents. When you are firmly in possession, get up and decide your next play.

|| || **drive off your foot** ▶   ▶   **extend to your maximum** ▶   ▶   **roll forwards** ▶   **protect the ball** ||

|| Two vertical lines iindicate a pause for holding and checking your position in preparation for your next move.

▶ The triangle indicates continued movement in the sequence.

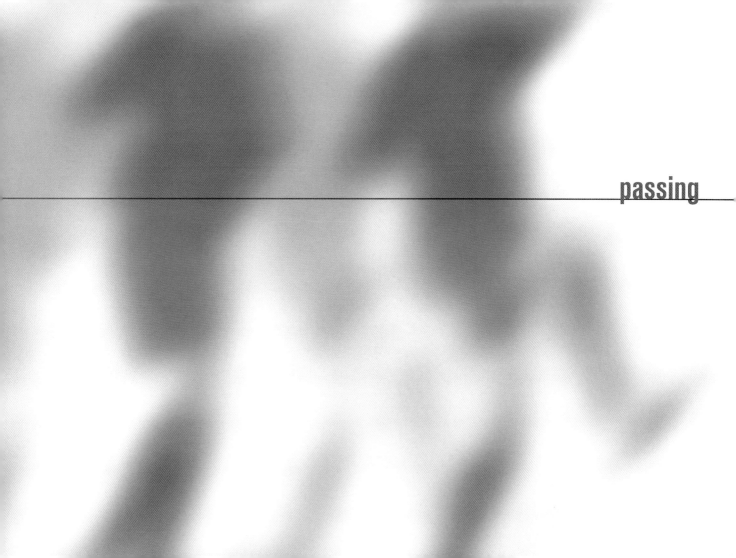

passing

control and side foot pass

The aim of this manoeuvre is to receive the ball from another player, bring it under control, then pass it on again. The inside of your foot offers the widest surface to make contact with the ball, so pass with this part as it will give you more accuracy. Note that this player is left-footed.

● Keep a close eye on the ball as it comes towards you. Keep your arms out to your sides, away from your body, for good balance.

● Start to swing your arms as you run to the right side of the ball. Then side step to the left of it. Getting your body to the line of the ball is crucial.

● You may need to side step twice before you are in the correct position. Stay on your toes all the while as this will help you keep your balance.

● Once you are in the right position, plant your right leg firmly to a stop, then turn out your left leg out so you stop the ball with your inside left foot.

● When you have got the ball under control, step back with your left leg to get ready for the outward pass.

● Use your arms to give your body the momentum it needs to carry through with the pass.

● Aim to pass the ball back in the direction it came from with your left foot. Practise this skill with both feet, so you can improve on your least favourite foot.

make contact ❙❙ ▶ ▶ **follow through** ❙❙

control and outside foot pass

This is similar to the side foot pass, but instead of using the inside of your foot to pass the ball, you need to use the outside part of your foot. When practising with a partner, try to keep the ball low to make control easier.

● Face side on as you start your run towards the oncoming ball. Just before you reach it, side step to your left to get in line with the ball.

● Your touch on the ball should place it in front of you. You will now be able to step into the next part of the pass and the ball will not be stuck underneath your feet.

● Put your right foot all the way down, then take a step forwards with your left foot.

● Aim to strike the ball with your right foot, which means you need to bring your leg across your body.

● As you lean forwards, point your foot slightly to the left of the ball. Once you have struck the ball with the outside of your foot, look up towards your target.

● This type of pass should create some spin on the ball, which will make it curve from left to right.

● Try to maintain your composure and keep your upper body loose and relaxed as you follow the kick through.

control & change feet

To avoid an oncoming defender, you need to be able to change the direction of the ball's play. To do this, practise receiving the ball with one foot then passing it on with the other. Changing feet becomes very important once you start dribbling the ball.

● Try to get up on your toes as you step up to the oncoming ball. Don't take your eye off the ball. As the ball approaches, decide which foot you want to control it with to take it in the direction you want.

● Once the ball is in easy reach, plant your right foot down and stretch out with your left leg. Turn your left toes outwards to catch the ball on the inside of your left foot.

● Bring the ball under control, then take your left leg forward, placing the foot down slightly across your body.

● To change direction, turn your shoulders to the right. Keep your eye on the ball as you do so.

● Pick up your right leg and turn the toes outwards so you can kick the ball with the inside of your right foot.

● Look towards your pass and then back to the ball as you move to kick it. Strike the ball with the side of your foot for accuracy.

● Don't forget to use your upper body as you follow the kick all the way through as smoothly as possible.

change direction ⏸ ▶ ▶ **follow through** ⏸

lofted pass

Getting height on a stationary ball is useful when you need to pass it into attacking areas, with the aim of scoring a header into the goal. It's also good for long distance passing.

● When striking a dead ball, look at your intended target, then begin to approach the ball.

● Gauge the distance between yourself and the ball as you run towards it. Swing your arms to give you some momentum and balance.

● Once you are close enough, look back down as you address the ball. Aim to get your non-kicking foot beside the ball.

● As you approach the ball, take your right leg back and prepare to make the loft kick. Begin to lean back.

● Keep your eye on the ball as you use the instep of your right foot to strike the underneath of the ball.

● Lean back with your upper body to give your kick more power and the ball more loft. Take your arms up out to your side to help with balance.

● Follow through by bending your left knee as you raise your right foot and leg as high as possible. This will help to give the ball height.

distance throwing in

To achieve a long distance throw, hold the ball high above your head, keeping your elbows straight. This will allow you to harness the power in your shoulders and throw the ball a greater distance. Try to make the throw a continous, smooth action. Keep your feet behind the line and both hands on the ball.

● Use both hands to hold the ball firmly out in front of you. Look towards your intended target.

● Take a step forward towards the throwing in line with your left leg as you raise the ball above your head.

● Take another step in with your right leg, then brace your arms and bring them as far back as possible behind your head to create a catapult effect.

● When you bring your arms forwards again, the whole of the back and upper body should create an elastic effect to power the ball as it uncoils and straightens.

● Use your back foot to give your throw added power. Release the ball when it is at head height.

● Follow through by bending forwards with your upper body and bringing your arms down to your side. Make sure both feet are still behind the line.

● The strength and distance of the throw will be determined by the run up and the arch of your back. Keep both feet on the ground.

release the ball

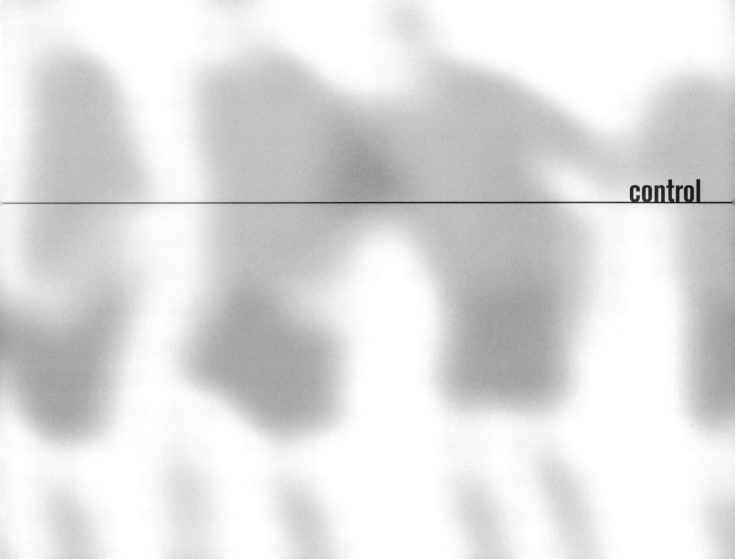

control

chest control

To bring a high, incoming ball under control, use your chest. Rather than presenting a completely rigid surface to the ball, let your body give a bit as the ball makes contact. This way you'll have greater control over the ball when it drops down to your feet.

● As you follow the incoming ball with your eyes, keep your body alert by bending your knees and elbows.

● Lean back, keep your arms clear of the ball, and stick out your chest in preparation for the arrival of the ball.

● Ease your chest back when the ball makes contact. This will help to cushion the ball and give you greater control. The ball should drop to the ground in front of you.

● Bring your left foot forwards for stability as you pick up your right foot in preparation for the kick.

● Keep your eyes on the ball as you lean forwards and bring your right leg back. Make sure your arms stay out to the side, as this will help with balance.

● Use the right side of your foot to pass the ball on. This is the widest surface you can hit the ball with, so it will make your pass more accurate.

● Raise your right leg high and lean back slightly to follow the pass through. Keep your rhythm smooth as you do so.

head control

Many beginners avoid heading the ball because they are concerned it will hurt. However, if you do the move properly, using the correct part of your head, it won't. The key is to absorb the energy of the ball by easing back a fraction when the ball makes contact. Then, when the ball drops down to the ground, it won't bounce away. Only practise heading balls for short periods of time.

● Once you have moved into position to receive the ball, step back onto your right foot. Keep your elbows bent with your hands up by your chest.

● As the ball comes towards you, lean back. Keep your eyes open and focused on the ball.

● Aim to make contact with your forehead. As the ball arrives, lean back further so your forehead absorbs the energy of the ball through the neck muscles.

● Direct the ball to your side by moving your head down towards your feet. Keep your eyes fixed on the ball.

● Use your right foot to get the ball under control, then prepare to pass the ball with inside of your right foot.

● Place your left foot alongside the ball, pointing in the direction of the kick. Swing back your right leg so you can bring the inside of your right foot in contact with the ball. Follow through with a smooth, flowing action.

make contact ▶   ▶   **prepare to pass** ▶   **follow through**   ‖

thigh control

The key to receiving the ball on your thigh is to keep your entire body supple and relaxed. When the ball comes into contact with your thigh, draw it away slightly so you soften its impact. Do not make the mistake of hitting the ball with your knee, as this will cause it to bounce away, out of control.

● Stand with your feet hip width apart and knees slightly bent in readiness for the oncoming ball.

● Keep your eye on the ball as you follow its path down towards you. Begin to lift up your right knee.

● By the time the ball makes contact, your thigh should be raised at a 45 degree angle to your body.

● Once the ball makes contact, collapse your thigh slightly to cushion the impact. Use your thigh to guide the ball down in front of you and to your left.

● As you bring the ball under your control, step in and turn towards your left. Lean forwards and bring your right leg back as you prepare to pass.

● Your left foot should be positioned alongside the ball, pointing in the direction you are aiming towards.

● Kick the ball with the inside of your right foot. Follow through by leaning back and looking up.

▶ **step in** ▶ **pass the ball** ▶ ‖

side foot control

To gain control of a high, lofted pass, you will most likely need to use both feet to settle the ball down onto the ground. Most players prefer to use one foot over the other, but you should try to develop the weaker foot because it comes in useful when learning to dribble the ball.

● As you prepare for the oncoming ball, make sure your body is relaxed and you are up on your toes.

● As the ball comes towards you, step forwards onto your left foot. Hold your arms out to your side to give you greater balance.

● Raise your right knee and turn your toes out so the inside of your right foot faces towards the ball. Step on the ball to control it.

▶   **stop the ball**   ▶

● The ball will most likely bounce a bit towards your left. Transfer your weight from left to right so you can pick up your left foot and use it to bring the ball back to the centre, between your feet.

● Step up to the ball with your left foot, ready to kick with your right. Your left foot should be beside the ball, with your toes pointing in the direction of your aim.

● As you prepare to kick, bring your right shoulder and leg back. This will help to give you a good swing so you can get some height on the ball.

● Focus on the ball as you use the inside of your right foot to kick it. Take your arms out wide as you follow through with the kick.

centre the ball   ▶   ▶   **follow through**   ‖

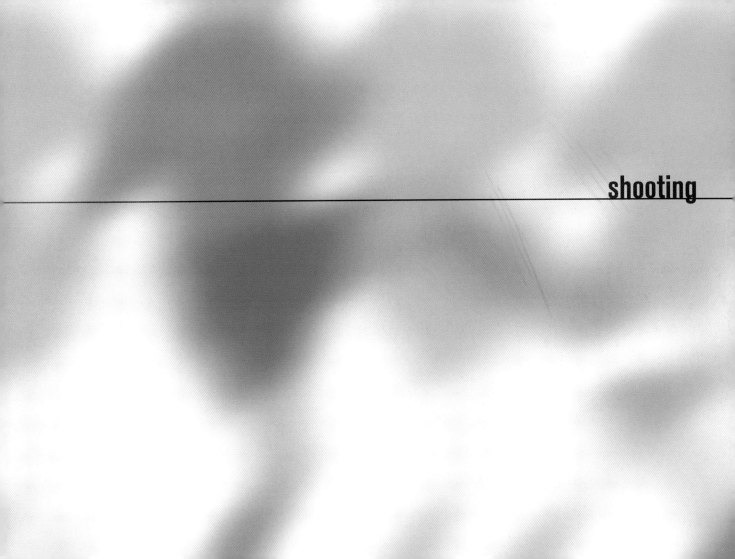

shooting

dead ball shoot

This technique is good for producing an accurate and powerful shot for a target a long distance away.

● You'll need to keep your eye on the ball once you begin the shot, so start by fixing a target in your mind's eye.

● Maintain your gaze towards the ball as you begin to step up to it. Swing your arms to give you momentum.

● Step up with your left leg so your left foot lies right up alongside, or even slightly in front of, the ball.

● As you bring your right foot in to make the kick, lean slightly over to the left and trail your right shoulder. This will give you more room to swing and therefore more power behind the ball.

● Try to strike the ball with the front of your boot so your laces make contact with the ball.

● To create curl and swerve, approach the ball from right to left, rather than straight on. Striking different sections of the ball will produce different flight movements.

● Follow the kick through by bringing your foot right up to waist height. Look up and swing with your arms to give the kick more momentum. For more power, jump off your left, non-kicking foot.

▶ **make contact** ▶ ‖ **follow through**

left side volley

shooting

The volley is the most powerful way to kick the ball, and requires not only strength but also precision, timing and balance. It's a great ball skill to have, especially if you need to shoot a goal with the ball approaching at waist height. This sequence shows a left-footed player, but you should always practise with your weaker side, as well as your preferred side.

● As the ball approaches, keep your eyes firmly fixed on it. You need to strike across the direction of the oncoming ball.

● If you use your left foot to kick the ball, lean away with your right shoulder as you step up for the shot. This will allow your striking foot to swing across your body at knee height.

● Pivot on the ball of your right foot as you take take the shot with your left. Keep your left arm out to provide good balance.

❙❙ watch the ball   approach   ▶   kick   ▶

● As you strike the ball with the instep (or laces), your whole body should swing across to the right to give the ball its momentum. To complete the follow through, step all the way around onto your left foot.

● You can practise this skill with a partner, who throws a ball towards you. Remember to swap positions after a couple of tries.

● If you are throwing the ball in, keep both feet firmly planted on the ground, bend your knees and hold the ball with both hands.

straight volley

shooting

A straight volley involves kicking the ball back in the same direction as it arrived. It is often used when the ball has been cleared by a goalie or defender. Do not lean back as this will cause the ball to rise up violently.

● Watch the ball as it comes in your direction. You need to get well behind the ball, so adjust your position accordingly.

● As you step up to the ball, put your arms out to the side to help you keep your balance.

● Keep your eyes fixed on the ball as you swing your right arm back and raise your right knee up high. You should hit the ball with the front of your foot so that your laces make contact with it.

● Keep the angle of your kicking foot slight so you create a smooth, straight path with the ball. Follow through by raising your kicking leg high and then stepping forwards onto it.

● If you are throwing the ball in, keep both feet firmly planted on the ground, bend your knees and hold the ball with both hands.

● You can also throw the ball in underarm to your partner. Do not make the throw too hard or fast.

shot from side delivery

Receiving the ball from a side-on pass and then shooting with just one touch requires a lot of skill. The key is timing your steps and the shot with the arrival of the ball. It may seem tricky, but with practise, it is definitely achievable. Note that this player is left-footed. If you are right-footed, simply swap the feet instructions.

● Timing is crucial for this manoeuvre so you need to watch the ball closely as it comes all the way into your feet.

● As the ball comes close, step up with your non-kicking leg (in this case, your right leg).

● Allow the ball to come across your right foot before it comes into contact with your left foot.

● Keep your eyes firmly on the ball, your arms out to the side and elbows behind you as you aim to shoot with one touch.

● Bring your right shoulder fowards and your left arm back as you put some momentum into the kick.

● Aim to strike the ball slightly across your body. Once you have kicked the ball, follow through by stepping forwards onto your left foot.

● As you steady yourself, look up to see if the ball has reached its intended target. This shot is difficult to achieve at first, but gets easier with practice.

make contact ▶ ❚❚ ▶ ❚❚

getting past opponents

step over/half scissors

This technique allows you to bypass your defender by putting him or her off balance. You need to have good ball control and be able to dribble quickly from side to side. Performing this at the right distance from the opponent is crucial; too far away and it will be ineffective, too close and you will get tackled.

● Crouch over the ball, keeping your arms slightly out to the side to protect the ball from other defenders.

● When you are about one to one and a half metres in front of the defender begin the move. If you are too close you will be tackled and if you are too far, the feint won't be effective.

● Get down low and bend your left knee as you make an exaggerated move towards your left.

protect the ball ▶ ▶ **feint to left** ▶

● To feign the movement you need to step over the ball, rather than kick it, and quickly power to the other side.

● Use the toes of your right foot to push the ball to the right of the defender, then follow on towards your right side.

● By doing this you will have hopefully put the defender off balance. Before he can regain his composure, you can move forward with the ball.

● Once you have passed the defender, accelerate away and make a pass or shoot at goal.

▶ **move to the right**　　▶ **bypass defender**　　▶ **pass the ball on**　　**II**

shoulder drop

The aim of this manoeuvre is to put your opponent off balance. By dipping your shoulder, you are enticing him to lean over one way. You, however, change direction by moving the ball with the outside of your foot. This is a left-footed sequence.

● Keep your eye on the path in front of you as you nudge the ball forwards with your left foot.

● Alternate your focus between the ball and the defender as you continue dribbling the ball forwards, gathering speed.

● When you are about a metre away from your opponent, begin the move by stepping onto your right foot.

edge forwards   ▶   ▶   **step onto right foot**   ▶

● As you shift your body weight onto your right leg, dip your right shoulder. This will entice your opponent to also lean to the right in a bid to tackle you. The more exaggerated the dip, the more effective you will be.

● When your opponent moves to the right, you should quickly change direction to the left

● As you nudge the ball to the left, your opponent will be struggling to regain his or her balance.

● You should now be past your opponent, in full possession and control of the ball. Accelerate away and pass or shoot at goal.

move towards the right ▶ **change direction** ▶ ▶ ‖

This is another way of outwitting your opponent and getting the ball past him or her. It involves moving the ball quickly from side to side, creating sudden changes of direction to your path.

● Keep your eye firmly on the ball and your arms out to your side, which will help you to maintain your balance.

● Continue focusing on the ball as you use the outside of your right foot to edge the ball slowly forwards.

● Lean towards your left side and reach out with your right foot so it is resting on the ball's outer surface.

● Continue leaning to your left as you roll your foot over the ball. You should roll the ball with the base of your foot so it moves from right to left.

● This sudden rolling moving will fool your opponent, who has moved to your left in the expectation that you play the ball on this side.

● Once you have rolled the ball to your left, lean forwards as you play the ball with your left foot.

● You should be clear of any defence now and able to play the ball to the left of your previous defender and accelerate away.

step over

Another way of beating a player is to transfer your body weight from left to right (or vice versa) and step over the ball. This gives the illusion that you are going to play the ball with one foot, but you actually step over the ball and use your other foot instead.

● Push the ball forwards with your right foot. Crouch over the ball as you stay low to the ground.

● Keep your eye on the ball, looking up every now and then to check your opponent's position on the field.

● Move your left leg towards the ball as if you are intending to kick it with your left foot. Instead, take your left leg over the ball.

● Once your left foot is over the ball and firmly planted on the ground, transfer your body weight and play the ball with your right foot.

● With the defender fooled and off balance, you are now free to take the ball off and around the defender.

● Play the ball away from the defender with your right foot. Stay low to the ground.

● Keep your eyes firmly fixed on the ball as you knock the ball into a good stride pattern.

turns

stop turn

This is the best turn to use when you have a defender running alongside you and you want to shake him or her off by changing your direction suddenly.

● Keep your eyes on the ball as you dribble it forwards, maintaining close control over it. Look up every few strides to check your position.

● As your opponent draws close to you, keep him or her guessing as to what you are planning to do.

● Put your leading right foot on top of the ball to stop it suddenly. Use your momentum to step over the stationary ball.

● Plant your right foot in front of the ball, then pivot on it as you bring your left leg around in a clockwise direction.

● You should be turning your body so that your back is facing towards your opponent. Lean back in towards him or her.

● Regain your balance as you push off the left foot and use the right foot to dribble the ball forwards.

● As you accelerate in the opposite direction, your opponent will, hopefully, still be moving in the original direction of play.

turn around ▶ **dribble in the opposite direction** ◀

drag turn

This manoeuvre is similar to the stop turn, but has the added advantage of pushing the ball back in the opposite direction before you turn around, giving you a head start.

● As you dribble the ball forwards, take your arms out to your side to help you maintain your balance.

● Stay firmly focused on the ball as you continue nudging it forwards. Look up every now and then to check your position. Try to keep the defendant guessing as to what your next move will be.

● When you have touched the ball forwards with your left foot, bring the right foot over the ball.

● Make contact with the ball by placing your right foot on the ball. Make sure the heel of your right foot is touching its surface.

● Your left foot should be firmly planted on the ground as you lean forwards and drag the ball back with the sole of your foot, working from heel to toe.

● Put the right foot back down onto the ground, then pivot on the ball of your right foot as you turn around in a clockwise direction.

● Once you are facing in the opposite direction, drive off the left foot to accelerate and follow the ball.

▶ **drag back** ‖ **begin to turn around** ◀

cruyf turn

This turn relies on you fooling your defender into thinking you are going forwards when, in fact, you are making a quick about-face manoeuvre in the opposite direction.

● Keep your focus on the ball and your arms out to your side as you dribble the ball forwards.

● Crouch down low, making sure your shoulders are well over the ball to protect it from any tackles.

● Gather speed while keeping control over the ball. When you are about a metre in front of your opponent, touch the ball forwards with your left foot and pretend to kick the ball with your right.

dribble forwards ▶   ▶   ▶

● Instead of kicking the ball, use the toes to hook the ball and pull it around in the opposite direction.

● Lean towards your left as you pull. Your right leg pulls the ball in towards your left side.

● Swivel on your left foot as you turn your shoulders and then your whole body anticlockwise to the left.

● Push off with your left foot as you lean forwards over the ball and accelerate in the opposite direction.

outside hook

This turn is used when you need to make a direction change because there is an opposing player tracking you on your inside. It involves taking the ball back in the opposite direction by keeping your body between the ball and the opponent.

● As you nudge the ball forwards, keep your arms out towards your side and your gaze firmly on the ball.

● Once you have dribbled the ball with your right foot, place the right foot down behind the ball.

● Keeping your eyes on the ball, place your left foot to the left side of the ball, then start to bring your right foot around to the left of the ball.

● Transfer your weight onto your left leg as you lean over to your left side o help you manoeuvre your foot round the ball.

● Use the outside of your right foot to hook behind the ball and flick it in the opposite direction.

● Once you have flicked the ball back, follow through by pivoting on the left foot and stepping your right foot around in a clockwise direction.

● Lean forwards and drive off the left foot as you propel yourself in the other direction. Use your arms to help you gain some momentum and accelerate away.

flick the ball   **step around**   ‖ **move in the other direction**   ◄

inside hook

This turn should be used when you need to change direction because an opponent is on your outside. It involves taking the ball in the opposite direction by keeping your body between the ball and your opponent.

● Keep your eyes fixed on the ball and your hands out to your side as you nudge the ball forwards.

● Dip your left shoulder slightly as you lean to the left and dribble the ball with your right foot.

● Then, step your right foot behind and to the right of the ball. Keep your eyes fixed on the ball.

● Place the left foot beside the ball and to the right. This move should happen quickly so it comes as a surprise to your opponent.

● Lean towards your left as you turn your body in an anticlockwise direction around the ball.

● Use the inside of your right foot to hook the ball and kick it back in the opposite direction to its original path.

● Look up to check whether your path is clear and accelerate off your left foot as you move back in the opposite direction.

▶   **hook the ball**   ❚❚   ◀

heading the ball

power header

To get power behind a header you need to use the whole of your upper body, particularly your neck muscles. Don't forget to arch your back and thrust your shoulders forwards as you reach for the ball.

● Rock forwards onto your left foot a couple of times as you build up momentum for the header.

● As the ball approaches, judge its distance so you can time your rocking with its arrival. You are aiming to strike the ball with your forehead.

● Keep your eyes open and begin to arch your body forwards to meet the ball. Aim your forehead at the middle of the ball.

● Once the ball makes contact with your forehead, arch your back and use the whole of your upper body to power it forwards. Aim the ball towards your partner's chest.

● Take turns throwing the ball and heading it. Do not do more than 20 headers at one time.

● Throwing the ball underarm will provide a more accurate aim. Make sure you bend your knees and use both hands on the ball.

defensive header

heading the ball

These are used to defend corners and free kicks by aiming to head the ball away in a direction opposite to which it arrived. Heading the bottom of the ball gives height to defensive clearance.

● To succeed with a defensive header, it's important to attack the ball to get maximum distance on your header.

● To prepare for the header, rock back and forth, bending down at your knees so they act as a launch pad.

● Judge your timing so you power up to the ball just as it is coming towards you. Aim to hit the bottom of the ball with your forehead.

● As you make contact, extend your neck away from your shoulders to send the ball far and high.

● Aim to get some height on the ball by looping it to your partner so he or she can catch it above his or her head.

● The thrower should always be facing towards the sun. Keep your knees bent and use both hands to throw the ball.

make contact ▶

◀ **throw the ball in**

downward header

The downward header is a good technique to use when you are heading for a goal.

● Keep your eyes fixed on the ball as it comes towards you. You need to time your move to reach the ball at just the right time.

● Rock back onto your right foot to create a launch pad for your header. You can do this a few times to develop greater momentum.

● Use your arms for leverage as you launch yourself forwards. Aim to get your forehead above the ball. Plant both feet firmly on the ground to provide a solid base from which to make your header.

● Tilt yourself forwards to get above the ball, then tilt your head down so your forehead connects to the top of the ball.

● Add some power to the header by following through with the upper body. Tilt your head down so the ball heads towards the ground.

● If you stand with your feet apart, you can ask your partner to aim the header between your feet.

make contact ▶ **follow through** ❚❚ ◀

jumping header

When competing for an oncoming high ball, you will need to leap up high to get your head to the ball first. Try to get a good run up and use your whole body – bending your knees elbows and arching your upper back – to get the height you require.

- Keep your eyes on the ball as you take a run up towards it. Bend your knees as you prepare to spring up.

- Bend your elbows to use your arms for extra leverage as you jump up towards the ball.

- Bring your head back as you aim to strike the ball with your forehead. Keep your eyes open the whole time.

● To give your header some power, arch your back when you make contact with the ball. Make sure to bend your knees to cushion your jump back down to the ground.

● If you stand further back than usual, you will be able to throw the ball higher than normal. This will allow your partner to run up for the header.

● Throw the ball underarm to get more accuracy. Bend your knees and use both hands.

follow through ◀

running with the ball

running short distances with the ball

running with the ball

Dribbling the ball short distances is an important skill to master. You need to keep your eyes on the ball, but at the same time, be aware of your surrounding defenders and the route you aim to take.

● Keep your body crouched low over the ball, with your arms out to the side. Focus on the ball.

● Begin to move the ball forwards by tapping it firmly with the outside of your foot.

● Next, use the inside of your foot to propel the ball further forwards and keep it on track.

stay low　　　▶　　　move the ball forwards　　　▶　　　　　　▶

● Keep your eyes firmly fixed on the ball, but try to maintain an awareness of who and what is around you.

● Try to keep the ball no more than 30 or 40 centimetres away from you. Any further and you may quickly lose control over it.

● As you continue to tap the ball with the inside and outside of both feet, dip your shoulders and bend your knees to help you shift your weight from side to side.

● When you become more confident at dribbling the ball, quicken your pace. As you build up speed, you can lift your head up to see around you.

develop pace ▶ **shift your weight** ▶ **II**

running long distances with the ball

Knowing when to run with the ball and when to pass it is what makes a good football player. Running a long distance requires only a few touches of the ball. As well as pace, you will need good control of the ball. Look up occasionally to avoid tackles and assess the situation.

● Start by focusing your eyes firmly on the ball in front of you. Try to keep your shoulders over the ball and your arms out to your side to protect it from defenders.

● Push the ball forwards a good distance, using either the inside or outside of your foot, depending on your intended path.

● Make sure your first touch of the ball is a good one because this will create the stride pattern for the next touch.

protect the ball ▶ **touch the ball** ▶ ▶

● Accelerate your pace. Bend your elbows and swing your arms back and forth to create momentum.

● Each touch of the ball should push it a good distance to maintain your stride pattern.

● As you touch the ball forwards, look up so you can think about your final pass.

● Do not push the ball too far forward, or you will run the risk of losing control over it.

accelerate ▶ **shift weight** ▶ **‖**

dribbling with both feet

Most players have a favourite foot with which they prefer to play the ball. But don't neglect developing your weaker foot. Although difficult, being able to use both feet is a very useful skill when it comes to warding off defenders while running with the ball.

● Crouch down low to the ground with your shoulders over the ball. Start by tapping the ball forwards with your outside right foot.

● Keeping your body over the ball, step in with your left foot and use the outside part to move the ball along.

● As you shift from side to side, dip your shoulders. This will help you transfer your body weight.

crouch down low ▶ **use left foot** ▶ **shift your weight** ▶

● Step in with your right foot again and use the outside part of the foot to move the ball.

● Keep your arms out by your side and bent at the elbows to help you with your balance.

● Now use the outside of your left foot again to move the ball. The ball should be moving forwards in a shallow zigzag manner.

● To maintain control over the ball, keep your knees bent and your eye firmly focused on the ball.

goalkeeping

basic catch

Standing between the posts in the line of fire is not everyone's idea of fun. But goalkeeping is vital for the game and requires not only bravery, but also agility, sound judgement and good kicking skills. You should aim to always keep up on your toes and be aware of your position in your goalkeeping area – don't remain on your goal line. Always wear the necessary goalkeeping equipment for games, and try to wear gloves during practice.

● Stand about a metre away from the goal line. Bend your knees and keep your weight evenly distributed over the feet. Bend your elbows and keep your hands out in front of you.

● As the ball comes close, step towards it. Keep your eyes firmly fixed on the ball as you reach up with both hands to catch it.

stand steady ▶ **reach up**

● Spread your palms wide so your hands make a 'W' shape. Once you make contact with the ball, tighten your grip so you are holding it firmly.

● Continue to cradle the ball tightly with both hands as you bring it in towards your chest.

● Keep the ball close to you as you step out and turn your head, first to the left and then to the right, as you prepare to pass the ball.

● Once you have looked both ways and found a suitable space, you can either kick the ball or throw it out to one of your players.

grip the ball   **‖**   **look both ways**   **‖**

catch above head

For a high oncoming ball, you
will need to adjust your
position so you can leap up
into the air with your arms
outstretched above you.

● Keep your body supple as you
prepare yourself for the shot. Bend
your knees and elbows, and maintain
your focus on the ball.

● Once the ball is in the air, step
forwards well away from the goal line.
You don't want to stumble back with
the ball and accidentally cross it.

● Reach up with both your hands,
making sure the palms are spread
wide apart and are facing the ball.

● Step onto your toes as you stretch your body high into the air. You should be aiming to catch the ball at its highest point.

● Once you have caught the ball, draw it in quickly towards your chest with both hands.

● With the ball safely in your possession, look around for opportunities to pass the ball.

● Take your right shoulder back and bring your left one forwards as you prepare to throw the ball out.

dive goalkeeping

Sometimes you do not have time to get your whole body in front of the ball so you will need to dive towards it.

● Stand about a metre in front of the goal line with your weight evenly distributed on both feet and your hands by your waist.

● Try to anticipate which way the shot is going before you commit to one side.

● Once you have committed yourself to a side, aim to get your hands on the ball as soon as possible. Drive off the opposite foot to your intended direction and propel your whole body across the goal.

● Keep your eyes on the ball all the time you are reaching for the ball. Your hands should remain in the basic 'W' shape throughout the dive.

● Stretch your body as far as you can to reach for the ball. Keep your eyes open and fixed on the ball.

● Aim to get both hands firmly on the ball. Keep your head as upright as you can, as this will help to prevent you hitting your head on the ground.

● Gather the ball into your body as quickly as possible Remember to roll forwards onto the ball. Don't lie back – you could roll over your own goal line by accident.

● Use your whole body to protect the ball from nearby opponents. When you are firmly in possession, get up and decide your next play.

extend to your maximum ▶ ▶ **roll forwards** ▶ **protect the ball** ❚❚

index